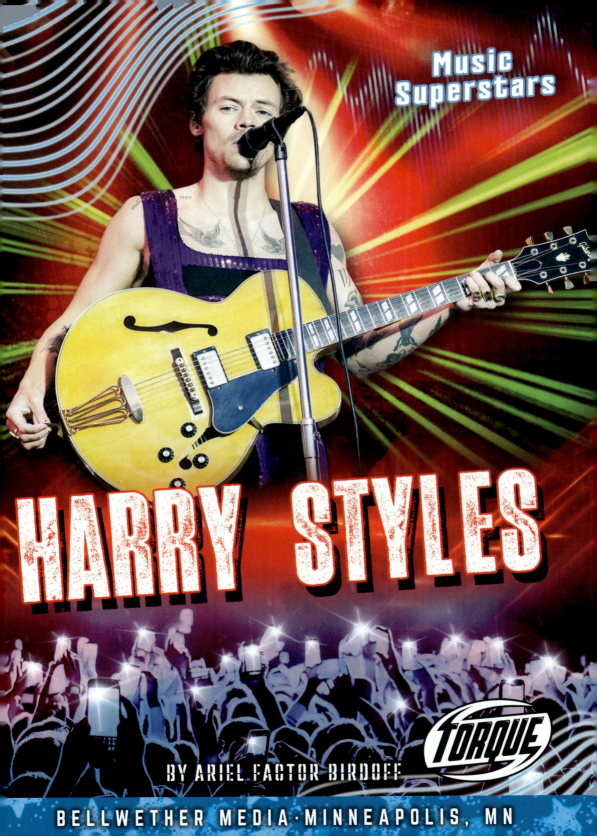

Torque brims with excitement perfect for thrill-seekers of all kinds. Discover daring survival skills, explore uncharted worlds, and marvel at mighty engines and extreme sports. In *Torque* books, anything can happen. Are you ready?

This edition first published in 2025 by Bellwether Media, Inc.

No part of this publication may be reproduced in whole or in part without written permission of the publisher. For information regarding permission, write to Bellwether Media, Inc., Attention: Permissions Department, 6012 Blue Circle Drive, Minnetonka, MN 55343.

Library of Congress Cataloging-in-Publication Data

Names: Birdoff, Ariel Factor, author.
Title: Harry Styles / by Ariel Factor Birdoff.
Description: Minneapolis, MN : Bellwether media, 2025. | Series: Music superstars | Includes bibliographical references and index. | Audience: Ages 7-12 | Audience: Grades 4-6 | Summary: "Engaging images accompany information about Harry Styles. The combination of high-interest subject matter and light text is intended for students in grades 3 through 7"– Provided by publisher.
Identifiers: LCCN 2024047010 (print) | LCCN 2024047011 (ebook) | ISBN 9798893042658 (library binding) | ISBN 9798893043624 (ebook)
Subjects: LCSH: Styles, Harry, 1994–Juvenile literature. | Singers–England–Biography–Juvenile literature. | LCGFT: Biographies.
Classification: LCC ML3930.S89 B (print) | LCC ML3930.S89 (ebook) | DDC 782.42166092 [B]–dc23/eng/20241008
LC record available at https://lccn.loc.gov/2024047010
LC ebook record available at https://lccn.loc.gov/2024047011

Text copyright © 2025 by Bellwether Media, Inc. TORQUE and associated logos are trademarks and/or registered trademarks of Bellwether Media, Inc.

Editor: Elizabeth Neuenfeldt   Designer: Josh Brink

Printed in the United States of America, North Mankato, MN.

TABLE OF CONTENTS

Singing in Style 4
Who Is Harry Styles? 6
A Karaoke Start 8
One Direction to Stardom 12
Treating People with Kindness 20
Glossary 22
To Learn More 23
Index 24

SINGING IN STYLE

It is the 2023 **BRIT Awards**. Dressed in a dazzling red jacket, Harry Styles performs his hit song "As It Was" to an excited crowd.

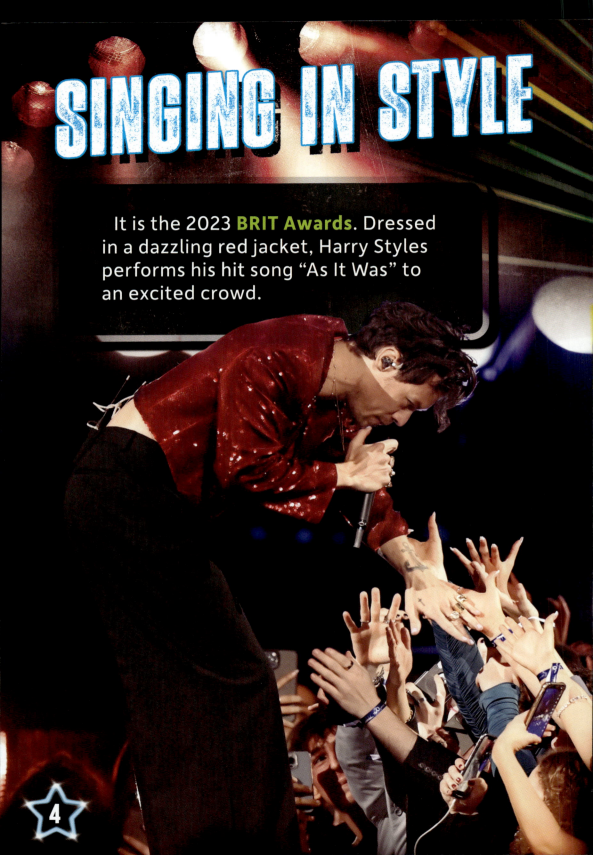

LOOKING GOOD!

Harry was the first man featured alone on the cover of *Vogue* magazine!

2023 BRIT AWARDS

"As It Was" goes on to win Song of the Year at the **ceremony**. Harry also wins three other awards. They include Album of the Year and Artist of the Year! Harry is a music superstar!

WHO IS HARRY STYLES?

Harry Styles is a British singer, songwriter, and actor. He was an original member of the popular boy band One Direction.

ONE DIRECTION

HARRY STYLES

Birthday	Hometown	Types of Music	First Solo Hit
February 1, 1994	Redditch, England	pop, rock	"Sign of the Times"

Later, Harry became an award-winning **solo** artist and famous **heartthrob**. He has performed all over the world. He is one of the richest musicians in the United Kingdom.

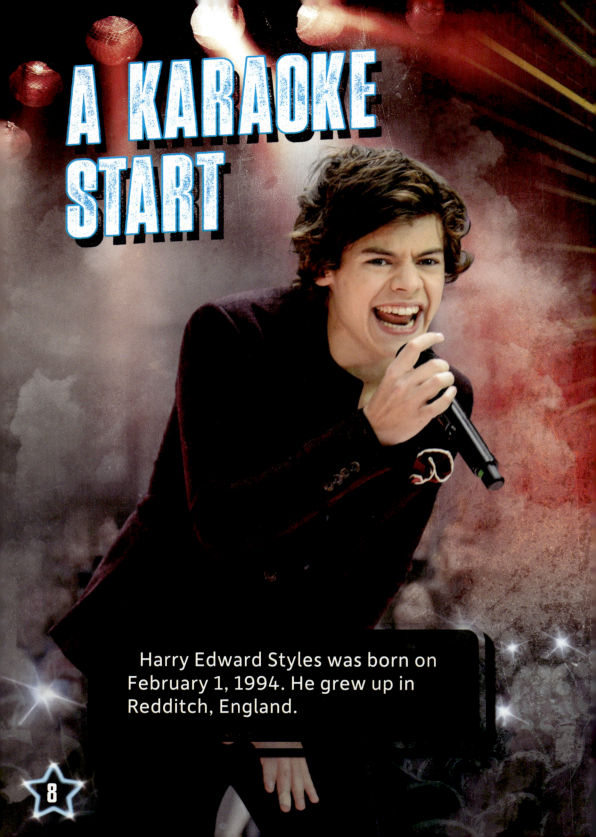

A KARAOKE START

Harry Edward Styles was born on February 1, 1994. He grew up in Redditch, England.

When he was a kid, his grandfather gave him a **karaoke machine**. Harry loved singing songs on it. He even recorded some of them! His first recorded song was Elvis Presley's "The Girl of My Best Friend."

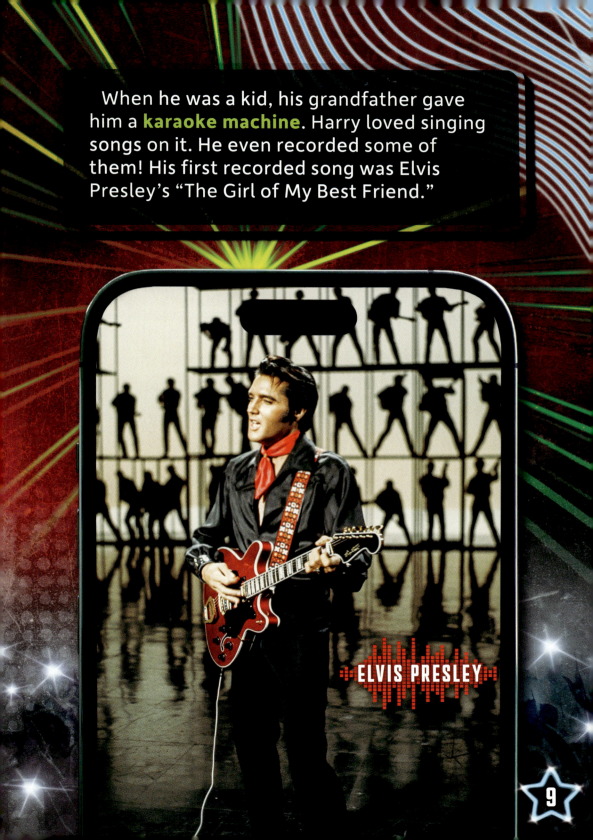

ELVIS PRESLEY

When he was a teenager, Harry was the lead singer of a band. When they came in first place at a local contest, Harry knew that he wanted to be a performer.

His mother said he should try out for *The X Factor* television show. Harry agreed.

HARRY ON THE X FACTOR

HARRY STYLES
Student, 16

FAVORITES

Animal
turtles

Colors
orange and blue

Food
tacos

Soccer Team
Manchester United

ONE DIRECTION TO STARDOM

In 2010, Harry competed on *The X Factor*. He did not reach the finals solo. But he teamed up with four other boys. They became One Direction. The band reached the finals. They won third place!

ONE DIRECTION IN 2010

"WHAT MAKES YOU BEAUTIFUL" RELEASE

TOP SONGS

One Direction has made many hit songs. They include "Story of My Life" and "Best Song Ever."

In 2011, One Direction signed with Syco Records. They **released** their U.K. number-one single "What Makes You Beautiful" on their first album.

One Direction released four more albums before taking a break. In 2016, Harry signed a solo **contract** with Columbia Records. He also launched his own **record label**. It is called Erskine Records!

His first solo single, "Sign of the Times," peaked at number one on the U.K. singles chart. It also hit number four on the *Billboard* Hot 100.

AWARDS
as of October 2024

4 MTV Video Music Awards

6 BRIT Awards

9 iHeartRadio Music Awards

3 Grammy Awards

RETURN TO THE X FACTOR

Harry got to perform solo on *The X Factor* stage in 2017. It was the first time since his original appearance!

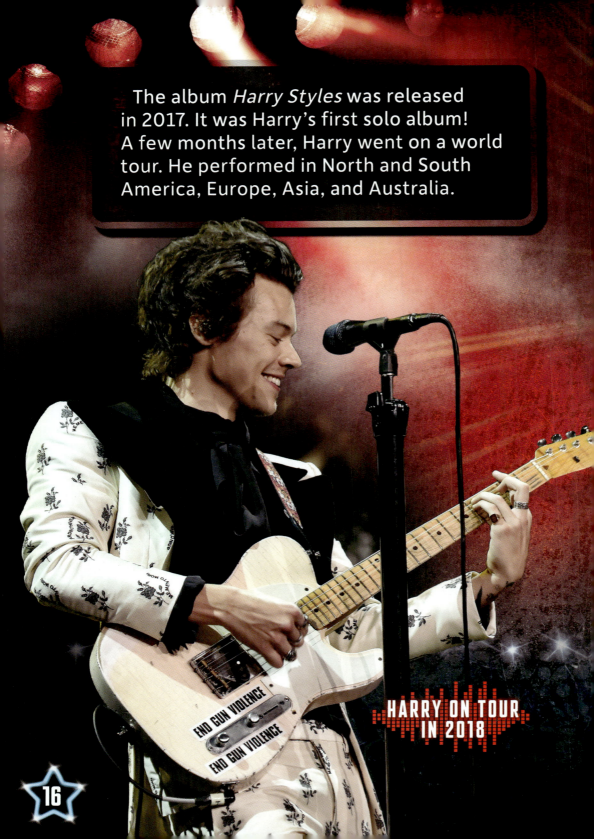

The album *Harry Styles* was released in 2017. It was Harry's first solo album! A few months later, Harry went on a world tour. He performed in North and South America, Europe, Asia, and Australia.

HARRY ON TOUR IN 2018

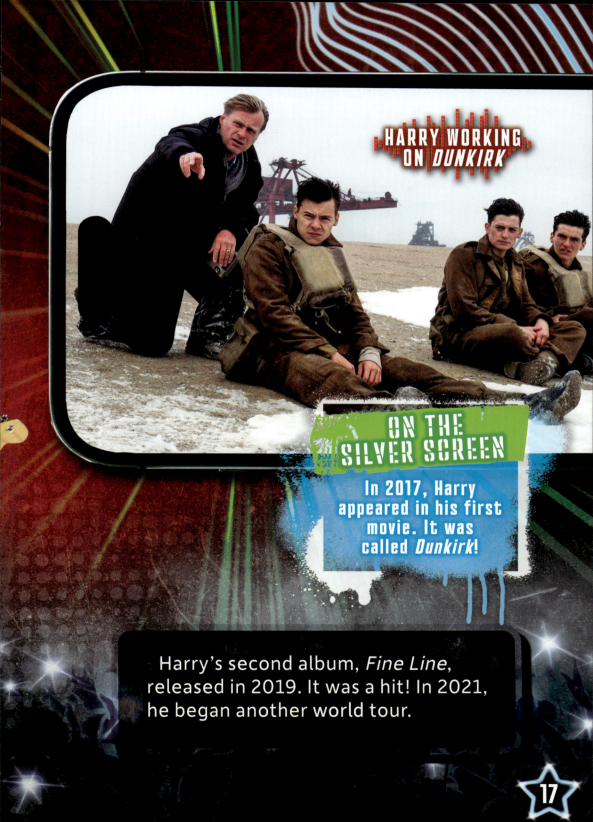

HARRY WORKING ON *DUNKIRK*

ON THE SILVER SCREEN

In 2017, Harry appeared in his first movie. It was called *Dunkirk*!

Harry's second album, *Fine Line*, released in 2019. It was a hit! In 2021, he began another world tour.

In 2022, his third album, *Harry's House*, **debuted**. It was number one in the U.K. and the United States.

In 2023, *Harry's House* won Best Pop Vocal Album at the 2023 **Grammy Awards**. It also won Album of the Year! Harry continues to be a music superstar!

A TALENTED SONGWRITER

Harry has helped write songs for other artists. He even wrote a song for Ariana Grande!

TIMELINE

– 2010 –
Harry tries out for *The X Factor*

– 2011 –
One Direction releases the song "What Makes You Beautiful"

18

2023 GRAMMY AWARDS

— 2017 —
Harry releases the album *Harry Styles*

— 2019 —
Harry releases the album *Fine Line*

— 2023 —
Harry wins his third Grammy Award

19

TREATING PEOPLE WITH KINDESS

Harry's fans, or "Harries," are **enthusiastic** and **diverse**. They love him for his talent.

LOVE ON TOUR PERFORMANCE

PLAYLIST

"Sign of the Times" (2017)

"Kiwi" (2017)

"Watermelon Sugar" (2019)

"Adore You" (2019)

"As It Was" (2022)

Harries also love Harry's kindness. Harry has spoken up for many causes. During his tour, Love On Tour, he raised over $6.5 million for **charities** around the world. Harry wants fans to treat people with kindness!

GLOSSARY

Billboard—related to a well-known music news magazine and website that ranks songs and albums

BRIT Awards—a music awards show held in England each year; BRIT stands for British Record Industry Trusts.

ceremony—a formal event for presenting awards

charities—organizations that help others in need

contract—an agreement between two or more people

debuted—was introduced or released for the first time

diverse—made up of people or things that are different from one another

enthusiastic—showing intense enjoyment

Grammy Awards—yearly awards given by the Recording Academy of the United States for achievements in music; Grammy Awards are also called Grammys.

heartthrob—a famous person known for their good looks

karaoke machine—a machine that plays instrumental accompaniments for singers

record label—a company that sells music

released—made music available for listening

solo—relating to music performed by one person

TO LEARN MORE

AT THE LIBRARY

Anderson, Kirsten. *Who is Harry Styles?* New York, N.Y.: Penguin Random House, 2023.

Andrews, Elizabeth. *Harry Styles: Everyone's Favorite Performer.* Mankato, Minn.: ABDO, 2024.

Schwartz, Heather E. *Harry Styles: Chart-topping Musician and Style Icon.* Minneapolis, Minn.: Lerner Publications, 2023.

ON THE WEB

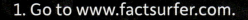

Factsurfer.com gives you a safe, fun way to find more information.

1. Go to www.factsurfer.com.

2. Enter "Harry Styles" into the search box and click 🔍.

3. Select your book cover to see a list of related content.

INDEX

actor, 6, 17
albums, 5, 13, 14, 16, 17, 18
awards, 4, 5, 7, 10, 12, 15, 18, 19
Billboard, 14
charities, 21
childhood, 8, 9, 10
Columbia Records, 14
contract, 14
Dunkirk, 17
Erskine Records, 14
family, 9, 10
fans, 20, 21
favorites, 11

Grande, Ariana, 18
Harries, 20, 21
One Direction, 6, 12, 13, 14
playlist, 21
Presley, Elvis, 9
profile, 7
Redditch, England, 8
songs, 4, 5, 9, 13, 14, 18, 21
Syco Records, 13
timeline, 18–19
tours, 16, 17, 20, 21
Vogue, 5
X Factor, The, 10, 12, 15

The images in this book are reproduced through the courtesy of: Press Association/ AP Newsroom, front cover (Harry Styles); Dungeon Hero X, front cover (lights); Taya Ovod, pp. 2-3; Debby Wong, pp. 2-3 (Harry Styles); Dave J Hogan/ Getty Images, pp. 4-5, 5; Michael Tran/ FilmMagic/ Getty Images, pp. 6-7; Ian West/ Alamy, p. 7 (infographic); Kevin Mazur/ WireImage/ Getty Images, p. 8; Michael Ochs Archives/ Getty Images, p. 9; jbrink, pp. 10 (*The X Factor*), 18-19 (albums), 21 (playlist); WENN.com/ Newscom, p. 11; Eric Isselee, p. 11 (turtle); New Africa, p. 11 (paint colors); Breyenn, p. 11 (tacos); AvocadoSt, p. 11 (Manchester United); Associated Press/ AP Newsroom, pp. 12-13; Dave Hogan/ Getty Images, p. 13; Charles Sykes/ Invision/ AP Newsroom, p. 14; Stefania D'Alessandro/ Getty Images, pp. 14-15; WFDJ_Stock, p. 15 (MTV Video Music Awards); Yui Mok/ Alamy, p. 15 (BRIT Awards); Tinseltown, p. 15 (iHeartRadio Music Awards); CarlosVdeHabsburgo/ Wikipedia, pp. 15 (Grammy Awards), 19 (Grammy Award); Kevin Mazur/ Getty Images, p. 16; TCD/Prod.DB/ Alamy, p. 17; Emma McIntyre/ Getty Images, pp. 18-19; Dabarti CGI, pp. 18-19 (timeline mixing board); WireStock/ Alamy, p. 20; Dia Dipasupil/ Getty Images, pp. 20-21; lev radin, p. 23.